LADY FAUSTUS

BY DIANE ACKERMAN

LADY
FAUSTUS
BY
DIANE
ACKERMAN

WILLIAM MORROW AND COMPANY, INC. NEW YORK 1983

I am grateful to the editors of the following periodicals for first publishing some of these poems: *The American Poetry Review, Black Warrior Review, Boogie-Woogie Review and Scriblerus Papers, Carolina Quarterly, Epoch, Kenyon Review, Michigan Quarterly Review, The New York Times Magazine, Oceans, Paris Review, Parnassus: Poetry in Review, Seneca Review,* and *Sites.*

"Cave Diving in the Tropics" received the Black Warrior Review Poetry Prize for 1981.

"Zoe" was selected for *The Pushcart Prize VIII: Best of the Small Presses,* edited by Bill Henderson.

Library of Congress Catalog Card Number: 83-61564

ISBN: 0-688-02396-7

Printed in the United States of America

First Edition

1 2 3 4 5 6 7 8 9 10

BOOK DESIGN BY LINEY LI

CONTENTS

III.

IV.

V.

VI.

VII.

LADY FAUSTUS

I.

❧ *A FINE,*
A PRIVATE
PLACE

He took her one day
under the blue horizon
where long sea fingers
parted like beads
hitched in the doorway
of an opium den,
and canyons mazed the deep
reef with hollows,
cul-de-sacs, and narrow boudoirs,
and had to ask twice
before she understood
his stroking her arm
with a marine feather
slobbery as aloe pulp

was wooing, or saw the octopus
in his swimsuit
stretch one tentacle
and ripple its silky bag.

While bubbles rose
like globs of mercury,
they made love
mask to mask, floating
with oceans of air between them,
she his sea-geisha
in an orange kimono
of belts and vests,
her lacquered hair waving,
as Indigo Hamlets
tattooed the vista,
and sunlight
cut through the water,
twisting its knives
into corridors of light.

His sandy hair
and sea-blue eyes,
his kelp-thin waist
and chest ribbed wider
than a sandbar
where muscles domed
clear and taut as shells
(freckled cowries,
flat, brawny scallops
the color of dawn),

his sea-battered hands
gripping her thighs
like tawny starfish
and drawing her close
as a pirate vessel
to let her board:
who was this she loved?

Overhead, sponges
sweating raw color
jutted from a coral arch,
Clown Wrasses
hovered like fireworks,
and somewhere an abalone opened
its silver wings.
Part of a lusty dream
under aspic, her hips rolled
like a Spanish galleon,
her eyes swam
and chest began to heave.
Gasps melted on the tide.
Knowing she would soon be
breathless as her tank,
he pumped his brine
deep within her,
letting sea water drive it
through petals
delicate as anemone veils
to the dark purpose
of a conch-shaped womb.
An ear to her loins
would have heard the sea roar.

When panting ebbed,
and he signaled *Okay?*
as lovers have asked,
land or waterbound
since time heaved ho,
he led her to safety:
shallower realms,
heading back toward
the boat's even keel,
though ocean still petted her
cell by cell, murmuring
along her legs and neck,
caressing her
with pale, endless arms.

Later, she thought often
of that blue boudoir,
pillow-soft and filled
with cascading light,
where together
they'd made a bell
that dumbly clanged
beneath the waves
and minutes lurched
like mountain goats.
She could still see
the quilted mosaics
that were fish
twitching spangles overhead,
still feel the ocean
inside and out, turning her
evolution around.

She thought of it miles
and fathoms away, often,
at odd moments: watching
the minnow snowflakes
dip against the windowframe,
holding a sponge
idly under tap-gush,
sinking her teeth
into the cleft
of a voluptuous peach.

CHRISTMAS
ON THE REEF

The ocean tugged my ribbon
free when I plunged,
so hair streamed like Medusa's
above me as I downfell
to gardens of hula-ing sea plumes
whose fibers oiled
the cool length of my body.
Curling round a feather,
hair straggled when I stopped,
and haloed like a dark gorgonian
rooted in the coral mesa ahead.

To my guide, hovering
over a purple sea fan
large enough to draft-cool an antelope,
I mimed *That gorgonian's nimbus*
of black hair's like my own.
His eyes chatted silently
behind his facemask.
Plucking at his arm, he swept a hand
wide to embrace the vista:
We have the sea within us,
he motioned, *our veins mirror the tides.*

My eyes watered
from that simple, stupefying truth
and, for a moment, the womb's dark tropic,

where swells tip monthly
and eggs lie coded as roe, lit my thought.

Pulling my mask aside,
I let the green Lourdes rinse
my cheeks, lave my make-up
into its flux, adding tear-brine
to the general swill,
then jammed hand to forehead
as if thought-struck,
blowing air down the faceplate
to recover.

Thanks to a sunclear day,
arpeggios of color
scaled the coral walls
and plummets hid flat, appaloosa fish,
beak-nosed turtles, and remudas
of sea horses livid with spawn.
Below us, skirty anemones
twirled a flamenco in the sand,
and, uphigh, our bubbles
grew silvery as sleighbells.
The guide checked his compass,
but home was everywhere.

❧ *CAVE DIVING*
IN THE TROPICS

A mile's drive from the ocean
through hip-high snarls
of liana, frangipani,
dark, thorny creepers,
and poison ivy keen with hell-sap,
the earth yawns
into a towering deep grotto
canted below ground,
with its own small sea
and boulder-strewn beach
where once, long ago,
Arawak Indians sheltered
under the vaulted ceiling
and bat-crusted walls,
knowing nothing perhaps
of what lay beneath
the water we ski into now
with masks and scuba-gear,
finding:

limestone spires of gothic beauty,
   high mesas, and mud-dark plummets
      where blind fish grope,
  their eye frames blank
        from long disuse,

tunnels twirling fine as bird bone
  through rock, trenches
    of chinchilla-soft mud,
      ceilings ripped like English muffins,
alcoves atwitch with gargoyles,
  batheads, fangs of limestone,
    spiderweb rock,
stalactites and stalagmites
        reeling at one another
    as if the walls were jousting,
      the halocline: a blurry film
where warm salt, and fresh cold, waters
    meet like dowagers,
flirt and cloy, but refuse to mate,
  and, above all, as you sink
    down the gourd-neck entrance
  deep into the cave's swollen belly,
rolling on your back,
      you see shimmering overhead,
clearer than any sweet dreams of reason,
  a fluke in the sunlight:
    a blue cathedral
  through whose stainglass window
sun gushes wide corridors of light,
    each searching the abyss,
        construing the gloom, while skindivers
    rise and fall among them
like mute choirs of the heavenbound.

    A scant moment, I hang
    in the twilight,
    watching the Creation scene

overhead: a vision
that could blister doubt:
and want to rise through the blue
on glittery sun drapes.

Beside me, a guide floats
hatchet-faced in the murk,
his gear an Arawak in profile.
The yellow stripe rimming his mask
sheds light:
a thin, hand-daubed glow,
and his cheeks look strong as plinths.
Will you come now,
he motions, *deeper into the cave,*
or will you stay here
with the uprushing foils of gold light?

Air bubbles pour above us
for long, dark seconds,
then flood the shallows
where light lies, and drift away
bright as doubloons.
What mattered to the Arawaks
was food, raincover, sun,
fresh water: their mysticisms
worked the oracle of Earth.
And mine? I wonder,
as, plunging away from the vision,
I fin down the cave
into the cold argument
of fresh and salt waters,
through firmaments
chillier than steel on ice.

Touch pioneers,
as we probe the cluttered avenues,
rainbows of rock, carp,
time-tortured pillars,
and plush wallows of womb-soft mud.

Too soon, round a bend
where stalagmites tower
rigid as bamboo,
we slip over a ledge
and find ourselves again
below the main hall's chandelier sun
that molds high darkness
into the cathedral
and, at our depth, pales water
from mink-brown to grey.
Through a silty blur
the guide motions
Up now, long enough.
He points to three divers
lilting toward the surface
on crystal beacons,
their angel-wings folded
tight as aqualungs.

Surface, the guide motions,
but I am already far away
where light breeds light,
spring herbs hearten my tongue,
and, out of the tropic vetch
I can hear, clear as a bell
over water, like an old spiritual,
life's green anthem.

❧ WHALE SONGS

Speaking in storm language,
a humpback, before it blows,
lows a mournful ballad
in the salad-krill sea, murmurs
deep dirges; like a demiurge,
it booms from Erb to Santa Cruz,
bog low, its foghorn a thick liqueur.

Crêpe black as a funeral procession,
the pod glides, mummer-deft,
through galloping brine,
each whale singing the same
runaway, roundelay tune:

Dry fingers rub, drag, drub
a taut balloon. Glottal stops. Pops.
Dry fingers resume, then, ringing
skeletal chimes, they ping
and rhyme—villanelles, canticles,
even a Gregorian done on ton tongues

as, trapped below the consciousness
of air, hungry, or wooing,
or lamenting slaughter,
jazzy or appalled,
they beat against the wailing wall
of water, voices all

in the marzipany murk they swim,
invisible but for their songs.

And often they raise high
as angels' eyes a refrain
swoony as the sea, question-mad
sad, all interrogatives, as if
trying to fathom the fathomless
reach from ladle-shaped ocean,
scurrilous surf, to breach-birth
upon beach and blue algae's cradle.

Sleek black troubadours
playing their own pipes, each body
a mouth organ, each shape a daguerreotype
of an oblate friar caroling,
they migrate, glad to chain rattle
and banshee moan, roaming the seas
like uneasy spirits, a song on their bones.

❧ AMPHIBIANS

All season we've tried
     to keep frogs from diving
  deeper into the chlorine-laced pool.
We run, skimmers twitching,
      to scoop them out; but no use.
  Three frogs dead in the filter
again today. Weightless things,
    water-pithed,
  their limbs cast open
(wider than in fieldlife),
       each muscle lax
     as a broken shade. Wan eyes
hug shut, as if in light contemplation.
    And out of sight,
  beneath the limp, leathery skin,
a genetic code mixes
       like alphabet soup,
     each tiny ladder split rungless now
for this final climb down to earth.

II.

❧ FLYING LESSONS

the view from the cockpit

Picture this. The plane's nose
high on the horizon,
as you arc the throttle open,
shoving its clenched fist
against the panel, and propeller blur
jumps to a sudden lit portal,
a stereopticon razory clear
through which runway and treeline
lunge close at a glide.
When the wheels dance, you drag
the stick back to your chest,
hold it rigid as a pharaoh's staff
until lift prospers, the ground dissolves,
flight is only an attitude in motion,

and you bank into nothingness,
climbing out on rungless ladders of air.

Picture this. Your wingtips
level with the horizon, and the propeller nub
boring into distance as you fly,
peeling the apple-fresh skin
from the planet. A plaid of green wheat
and yellow corn flat below,
and ploughed land pouring fast
on a hand-held globe, while you are motionless,
hanging like a crib toy on a spring,
cruising airily at 120 knots,
plus or minus 1,000 m.p.h.,
speed of the turning Earth,
plus 120,000 miles per second—blood hurtling
through velvet arteries, because your heart
is running like a hamster on a wheel.

Picture this. The hemisphere
of the instrument panel
racing into a perspective by Da Vinci,
as you swoop down the center stripe
of the runway, floating the last
few moments as a sail, or a kite
whose tail is rags of wind,
then chesting up until lift quits,
the last low sky falls from under you,
and you bounce on your shocks
like the stork or crane you will never be
in so glossy hard a carapace,

touch down with the round tedium
of wheels, and, stirred by the invisible,
settle deep and heaving, land-lucky,
on the right side of the ground.

❧ *NIGHT FLIGHT*

I.   At 12,000 feet, lights below
dot the blackness as if by rule,
fill our ever-arranging eyes
with sparkling motifs, a parole of order
vast, doping, and certain.

But suppose those gold temple bells
chime only in the mind.
Suppose that sheen is not geometry,
but mere angling, a peasant code
for the manorless void.

Then the apparent samba of geranium buds
banking to the light
would be an accident of faith
at a winter window.

Then ice honeycombed by chickenwire,
at daybreak, would be certain knowledge.
Then finding hieroglyphics
of sparrow tracks in the snow
would be cause to send telegrams
and unfurl all our flags.

Then the banana republic of the heart
would be everything.

II.   In the measured world below
lie unmapped constellations:
a winged camel, a milkman, a bee-clustered hive.
We will never name them
any more than the lit veils
on the skyline, or the gold membranes
as city lights float under us
the tracery of a fluorescent sea creature
on a moonless reef,
its backbone a tilted highway
glittering to the horizon,
neon hubs its organs and, in between,
the webbed tinsel of suburbia.

III.   Red lights in the cockpit.
A pilot cradles the wheel's two uplifted arms,
as unerring numbers
count backward to zero.
Their message is not new.
Drifting mindful somewhere
between the cities and the moon,
he watches numbers flicker,
as if to unravel them
and name their starry sum,
as if he could speak
the patois of sheer light.

⅔ CLIMBING OUT

FOR MARTIN

Blue fluid in my limbs,
momentum buoys me up
at take-off speed
as I lose ground for that puzzle
older than hearsay,
whose thraldom is a witless bird
navigating a meadow.

Then, heavily afloat,
I run the river rapids
we know only by effect:
smoke chugging downwind,
apple boughs swinging
their fruit like censers,
the heat mirage gusty
over Lake Cayuga
when, as now, it's flat steel
burning in the sun.

Below me, planes sit nose up
on the airfield, like energy resting.
Only cloud-puffs
high above. At 3,000 feet,
hard atilt, I stall,
and a warning buzzer screams
like a marmoset loose
in the cabin, the hull trembles,

shudders twice, like a woman
gently coming, then nestles
straight down toward quilted green
and bedrock, till I get wind
of the right attitude
for lying long on the air,
and land like someone tripping
over toys in the darkness:
stagger, lurch, recovered fall.

But late at night,
still awake in the birdless,
starless black of my bedroom,
I am the moon
rinsed with glitter,
floating full over a pokey
and obedient land,
I am motion unmasked
by a wafer of steel,
I am lift made visible,
I am a dancer
with starched coat-tails for wings,
I am the mouth of a river
whose source is the sky,
I am trembling and hot
from this power-on stall,
I am flight-luscious,
I am kneeling on air.

LINDBERGH

For Martin

Half his life he parachuted
from open cockpits in swamp fog,
and the other madly scouted
for where forced landings might work.
It was a tic, his mind painting crashes
as he flew (knowing pilots lived
only an average 900 hours aloft),
while at the same time eagle-eyeing
the stagnant autumn of the fields,
the village life which, as a farm boy,
he knew from the soil up,
to invisible rivers and culverts of air.

Lost, he'd buzz a country to see
what language the store signs spoke,
then reclimb the stairs of flight
to where he loved being
a hermit in a wooden cabin in the clouds.
He always carried a Minnesota boyhood
with him: that frozen winter quiet
so raw he felt a trespasser: the ocean
glaring white and inhuman far below
with enormous cakes of jammed ice,
as he steered alone by a compass
reflected in a lady's compact mirror.

He figured plane and heart would never quit
("How can a whirlwind stall?"),
never feared the wind streaming
at tornado speed over fuselage and wing,
nor the silk he would blossom
to the ground in so often,
as if rehearsing a final cocoon.
Above all, there was no mystery
to life's steepest thrill:
the stick vibrant in his hand,
a quart of stagger in the engine,
death stowed away in every bolt and copper wire,
all existence reaching from one horizon
to the next: spangled, perilous,
interflowing, dumb: in the same instant
supreme and completely without value,
hung on nothing, a few valves and a strut.

❧ SPACE SHUTTLE

By all-star orchestra, they dine in space
in a long steel muscle so fast it floats,
in a light waltz they lie still as amber
watching Earth stir in her sleep beneath them.

They have brought along a plague
of small winged creatures, whose brains are tiny
as computer chips. Flight is the puzzle,
the shortest point between two times.

In zero gravity, their hearts will be light,
not three pounds of blood, dream and gristle.
When they were young men, the sky was a tree
whose cool branches they climbed,
sweaty in August, and now they are the sky
young boys imagine as invisible limbs.

On the console, a light summons them
to the moment, and they must choose
between the open-mouthed delirium in their cells,
the awe ballooning beyond the jetstream,
or husband all that is safe and tried.

They are good providers. Their eyes do not wander.
Their fingers do not pause at the prick

of a switch. Their mouths open for sounds
no words rush into. Answer the question
put at half-garble. Say again
how the cramped world turns, say again.

III.

A RED CARILLON WHOSE BERRIES ARE BELLS

Because rain fell early
and long this summer, the yard
spawned hundreds of wild strawberries:
pendent hearts
below a canopy of leaves,
whose sawtooth edge we learned
to spot from afar,
but had to search for in sweat weather
when a porridge-white sun
made them fruit low
in the cool hutch of the grass.

/35

Some grew no larger than a wart,
or a kernel; others, fingernail-size,
we called "huge,"
weighing them on an open palm
like garnets
fresh from the lapidaries' quarter
in Tangier. Overripe,
some looked too bruised to touch,
but here and there
one grew perfect to form:
crusted with small seeds,
roly-poly, and symmetrical,
the textbook strawberry, *Fragaria*
(fragrant, sense-swilling),
ready for the margins
of a dictionary, and our plates.

Each day, before dinner,
we preened the lawn, crouching,
and swishing a gentle hand
over miniature orchards:
succulent, fat fruits
dragging on their stems
like bright red gizzards.
Those with teeth marks we left,
sensing disease,
and knowing how squirrels,
flushed up with nature's bounty,
bite once from a berry
and move to the next.
We dratted their waste,
but loved their insouciance.

Few hours soothed us more
all summer than those
        passed in the womb of the day,
                grazing like protohumans
    while squirrels foraged alongside,
            using us scarecrows
to ward off the cranky assaults
        of nesting wrens,
    and the rabbits were so tame
we could walk up
        and kick them in the rump.

        Indoors, the wild-strawberry jam
    we made with pectin,
            in rainbow-washed jars,
        fed us many breakfasts
on its rare, pungent curds,
        and the treat of merely being
            among the fruits of summer.

A CHAPTER FROM THE GARDEN

Where hot pipes
run under the pool deck
a garter snake
we tag "World Without End"
finds central heating
a boon to his aging hide.

He still likes to stroll
ten yards of bleached wood
to be swell
under the porte-cochere
of a cushion yew, or better yet
ladder up its needles
and coil right on top
in sunswilling rapture.

We find him there
each afternoon, an odalisque
in a striped caftan
resting his head
on one long elbow,
basking and feeding,
high, narrow, and handsome.

Nor does he mind
our infant-like ogling,
though a warm pea
offered to him on a fork tine
made him leap
down into the bowels of the bush
and whip under the pool deck
for quick cover.

Most days, tolerant to a fault,
he puts up with all
our menu mischief, barracuda stares,
poking and sarcasm,
treating us even
to his red forked tongue,
and Hindu rope trick
(where he disappears
down a coil of himself).

At sundown, he staggers
through the grass,
back to the slender missus
we often find at slink
beneath the wild orchids,
dashing and cool,
full of nobody's business,
a snatch of melody
in summer's unbroken hum.

❧ SPIDERS

The eight-legged aerialists
of the tented dawn are up and about.
One leaves a pale orchid,
its exoskeleton, on a twig,
while another fly-casts
against the wind, angling for the leaf
where it would sooner be;
the silk hardens, and it crosses,
tiptoe, the tiny span,
eager to turn mummies
from wing crisp to liquid caramel.

They dote on the tang of quarry,
however they nab it,
with trap door, or purse web,
or keen, jagged fangs,
holding out for that bronchial
shudder of the net, when something
angel-faint, ensnared and hairy
begins the tussle in rigged silk
that can start a greedy eye,
make gossamer hum and, at long last,
even their slack jams quiver.

❧ FREEING THE EVERGREENS

Weeks after an ice storm glazed
the poplar limbs and bearded everything,

even piled ghostly birdnests with chickadees
of snow, as if they'd been carved

for a champagne banquet, and jacketed
lean trees with ice (sunlicked,

they seemed to have streaming colds),
we sadly watched our cushion-yews

and evergreens hunch lower and lower
under freeform ice, heard tiny branches

crack like wishbones, saw the delicate
green feathers knuckle under,

pine-needles jell, like fossils into rock,
until neither of us could bear

the vicarious agony; panic ruled
and, setting out with brooms and shovels,

we thwacked the branches clean,
filled the yard with slagheaps of snow

as we dug out the bittersweet
and the matted ivies, lifting vines

snakewise over a broom handle
to fluff their ice-bedraggled creepers,

untied the weeping aspen's arms
and, out front, freed the evergreens

crouching under an impossible burden,
stoop-shouldered as pyramid builders

and nearly crippled for all their beauty,
one by one walloped icebergs to smithereens,

uncovering branchfork and tender shoots,
until at last the crushed limbs let fly,

danced in the air, flexed, stretched,
and we could amble indoors for a cup

of something hot, feeling as relieved
as the trees, and as silent:

not needing to voice an instinct
so blatant, so terror-packed, so close to home.

IV.

≈ *SLEEPING BEAUTY OF THE BRONX*

Last Friday, Dava Sobel, a science reporter from the *New York Times*, entered the human chronophysiology laboratory of Montefiore Hospital to begin 25 days as a research subject. She is cut off from the outside world. Freed of the constraints of the 24-hour day, her body is expected to establish its own biological day.

—*New York Times*, June 17, 1980

Dearest friend, dead to me
by time's present fiction:
    I read your plight weekly
        through the dream whorl of print,
    how they pox your face and arms

with high-strung electrodes, chart your blood-tides,
        stint you sunlight and chocolate.
A pheasant under glass,
                you are all alone
            yet never alone enough,
        glad-eyed by a legion of mute observers
drawn to the oasis of your vital signs.
        Even your spine begins lower now,
            with a rectal probe:
    in throwback irony, almost a tail.
Eeriest of all, you *feel*
        blood samples leeched from your veins,
            at random moments a quiet tugging.
How can I picture you,
        glass-frail in a glass burrow,
            neon blazing, and all your life-signs open,
with only a syringe's steel kiss
        on your birthday, yesterday,
though you told no one. Outside,
        in the fidget and bloom you crave,
        summer is like a new philosophy
    in the air, crammed with wild strawberries
and speckle-throated lilies,
            baby garter snakes
                lying like pencil leads in the grass,
    and the pool a single blue shudder
            where mallards
        bill-dip and ceremonially mate.

    Sleeping Beauty,
I read your *Times* article this morning
        and cried; one day,

through no fault of our friendship,
      we'll find ourselves
           a sleep apart forever,
betrayed by the green anthem we love
      and have plighted our word-troth to
           in such different ways,
exiled to the nightmare
      we ferry in our cells,
           rubbed to silence
                by the thickening waves.

❧ ICE DRAGONS

In a museum we find them
where they fell:
ichthyosaurus
with seven dragon whelps
in her belly;
sail-backed stegosaurus,
an armor-plated goon
wielding ratchety paws
and eye-coddling breath.

A pinafore of scales,
the sauropod toddles,
fanning its tail
through the mud
as it vamps
from bayou to sandpile,
teeth big as loaves,
a rosebud for a brain.

Another dips
a gravyboat head to drink,
while bird-monsters
on shoe leather wings
snuff the quickness
from a shrew.
Squat lizards spit bile,
and baggy-throated tots
trot after prey
with pipette-like claws.

Did they live on to test
Galahad and St. George?
Did they feel
the sudden whammy
of a global gasp?
We blizzard guesses
at their habitat.
We puzzle who
or what's to blame.
Only the bare bones
of a life remain.

IN A SCIENCE-
ILLUSTRATOR'S
APARTMENT

FOR SALLY LANDRY

Laundry the sign dins
by her front window,
as though the downstairs proprietor
eyed her at work
laundering a newt's bright web
with black stipples
to draw a fluxy view
of *Diemictylus viridescens.*
$500. For a Boston editor.

Upstairs: black washers,
rubbery as the eggs of a salamander,
sit unused in a box
while the faucet drips.
Mike sleeps; his drafting table
heaves with clutter—
books to design, new jazz albums, a cap. . . .

In the kitchen,
bananas hang bruiseless
on a string, sweetening
at the window sill.
Frameshop bills cling
to the refrigerator door

by an old swimming schedule
and a calendar cued
to outside events.
Her mother's recipe
for homemade prune bread
scents the counter
with the loaf it guarantees.
Leafy plants convalesce
in a south window.
Fishes, fin-perfect
in modeling clay, double
as *ad hoc* paperweights.
Pillageable books on everything.
Tea leaves, bay leaves.
Color charts of herbs,
sanddunes and wild flowers.
A stretch of purple columbine
drying in a noose.

Underfoot: sounds of argument
jar late into the night—
slamming, squalling, rhythmic dares.
An antique dealer
squeaks old wood
across the sidewalk,
puts out a bookcase,
like a tomcat, for the night,
curbs an unsellable chest
and three chairs:
alms for the thieves.
Bus stop and church chime
on the quarter hour.

Atoms of ink, points of dark,
her dots rim the fallow
pastures in a shape
to draw earwig, lousewort,
bottled gentian, porpoise,
australopithecine man,
then swap figure for ground:
not frog chassis now
but all the space frog-atoms
don't ignite, as if the frogs
penned on her foyer wall
were there just to hail
the universe of things not-frog.

Sally runs a barrette
through her loose, auburn hair,
fixes a blue, all-day
flame under the coffee
dripping through a filter
delicate as flesh,
watches a drop fall
into the quickening swill
black as the magic
of a million stipples,
preens her pen-shaft
with thin, deft fingers,
then chooses
the day's perfect nib.

❧ SILHOUETTE

Nightwing, you live in coffins
by day, a mortuary scribe
writing ads for guilt
abstract as leached bone,
with words like "perpetual,"
"always," and "everlasting,"
words too mineral
to use whole with a lover.
To feed your art,
you sell bereavement and brass.
But by night you fly.
Blood draws you out.
Your luxuriant fur glistens
in moonlight, as you steal women's souls.
Earthbound, they come
to sup with you in mid-air,
to give up reflection,
to learn to travel light,
as you roam the quiet spirals
of the world, squashing blossoms
against their pale necks.

Tonight, the air's a cool, slick whisper
to be flown, a benediction
of damp. Everything is at stake.
But all my pelts are twitching tight.
Already moths are beating

in my veins. Love, come drive
your purple fangs in steep,
and jolt me from my flesh tonight,
let me earn my wings.

WOMAN SITTING
UNDER A PALM

The sun shedding gold coins on the water.
And the trigger-happy wrens

cachinnating in a tree. And the silhouette
of a lizard spotlighted behind a palm frond.

And the tiny flies, jittery with life,
but so small when they land on anything wet

they die: a damp soda can, a sweaty arm.
And the sky iridescent and pale as a silkfish.

To the east, clouds lying thick and close,
wigwams spread against invisible mesas.

And the optical litany of sailboats at dockside,
across a bay sundazzled to the color

of running mercury. And the brogue
of a loud, irate dove on the clipped lawn.

And the wild morning-glory lassooing
a fence board with its tendrils,

holding only what's solid to its mongrel heart.
And then twilight, when the sun would set

down the water like a golden fish diving under,
and night pool with the dark luminosity

of a farm pond, as she trod the catwalk
between sleep and wakefulness. There are more cells

in one human body than stars in the galaxy.
Impossible. I'm possible, she thought.

TO VILLA-LOBOS IN WINTER

Night falls: a panther
springing.
On a black branch
swarmed over by stars,
an albino moon
rigs its parrot wings
then glides away
while icicle vines
drip in the sweat and tremble of the night.

Reptilian waterfalls
twist and freeze,
drooling ice down each rock face.
It would remind an Aztec
of his white-bearded gods
Bochica or the ousted Quetzalcoatl
who, vowing he'd return, did as Cortes,
a blue-eyed apparition on horseback,
wild for booty and Christ,
this time drawn from a far darkness
to these pagan depths
ropy with gold,
croaking with demons,
hot with gem flowers
set in green bezels
and blood swilled from vein to sky.

Tonight creeps
like the black diamonds on a snake.
Out of gorges, tortured winds
shudder and moan,
then fill with the hideous
panting of the gods.
Silver amaryllises,
the streetlamps bud high.
Mudgore cakes the road.
Under the parrot moon,
soughing a pink eye as it planes
over farm and settlement,
like a knife-edged idol
so chaste, so delicate,
there will be no waking from
this oblique dream of night.

❧ DAVID TISCHLER

Grandpa lay calm
as a principality between wars,
scented with bayberry rum
and flowers from a Caribbean
he had never been to.
Someone had trimmed the hair
from his nose and ears.

I asked for, and you gave me back,
so little, I thought,
leaning over the casket
to study his face with a surgeon's eye,
a grandchild's eye: tallow skin,
taut, persimmon lips
which sang songs and told jokes
in Polish and Hebrew
the few times I saw him
at weddings, funerals and bar mitzvahs.
That tall man
only and forever lengthwise.

Grandpa died one winter
that hit mild as sudden thaw
in the Rockies, when snow dance
melted before it struck
and the giant red geranium
in the Chinese urn outside
launched blossoms

among yellowing leaves.
Jackets left you shivering,
fur coats made you sweat,
and it seemed nothing alive
could be 90 years old,
nothing dead and beyond
midwinter barbaric
stymieing the pod
and the hibernating weasel.

One day my own father
would lie long in a box,
so I studied grandpa's large hands
caught in a rigid grip,
the dusty veins and pallor,
then, memorizing his last scent,
of a pomander on a shelf,
I made room for those
with keener needs to bridge.

❧ IN THE SILKS

The alarm sounds. The starting gates are empty,
there are no crowds, the track is clotted mud,
there is no finish line, there are no jockeys,
and, anyway, the horses are unride-able.

Nonetheless, at the bell all her muscles tense,
she leans to the jagged withers in her chair,
and her hand grips something wand-like and hard,
a man's body, or a memory, either one a whip.

⚡ ZOË

Ultimate immigrant,
who passed through the Ellis Island
of your mother's hips,
with a name slit loose
from its dialect of cell and bone:
welcome to the citadel of our lives.
We listened for the hoofbeats
(your heart) for nine months
and then your mother nearly died,
hospitably, to give you light.

Like an Hawaiian princess,
you are carried everywhere,
on a litter, in a carriage,
by the arabesque of one's arm.
Your feet have never touched ground.
You, who can't even roll over
when you want, creamy little tyrant,
control the lives of all around you.

Sound leaps from your face
and your ribs quake
each time the downy world chafes.
Last week, you first smiled
because grownups acted silly.
Things elude you, but you can grasp
absurdity already.

By mistake, you suck your wrist
instead of mother's nipple.
We laugh. With your operatic cries,
and Michelin-man pudge,
and seepages from below,
and eyes alert as twin deer,
you have no sense of self whatever.

Zoë Klein, goddaughter
with a hybrid name,
living in the soft new crook
of your mother's arm,
with a face like a Dalai Lama's
or a small Neanderthal's,
born out of a dream by two,

you live a dream by halves now:
slumbrous, milky-breathed.

In time, love will answer questions
you didn't raise. A belled marvel,
the cat of your inquiry, will stalk
through a world brighter
and more plural than you guess,
where a baby's fingerprints,
loopy weather systems, one for each tip,
will leave you spellbound

that matter could come to this.

❧ LADY FAUSTUS

I. Devils be ready! My curiosity
    stalks the outpost of its caution,
      and soon I'll swap anything
   from savvy to soul
      for one year's furlough
smackdab in the sleaziest lay-by
      you've got. Take me at my word,
   and now, if you like, before night
drives its purple fangs in deep.
      Like spilled pollen,
    sun coats the horizon: raw heat
      fitful as a cautery.
I, too, am burning with a lidless flame.

II.   Bluefall after twilight.
Mud and snow hyena-speckle the road.
    Through a cataract of frost
rimming the window, I browse
      a tiptilted moon, and shake loose
the predatory gaze of two planets.
    Jets crossing like motorboats
between the stars
      seem only a footstep from each
        port of call, a few fathoms perhaps
      to a way station
   tucked under the hem of night—

a viper's den, a Marrakesh
    full of low-life and baubles
mind never dreamed of, rickety hostels,
      banks and beaneries,
   phantoms that clack down the streets
like dice, artists and hucksters,
    grog-shops and depots,
the misguided, the lost, and the shanghaied.

III.   And in that circus mix
where merchants jaw with madmen
   neither men nor mad, I want to dawdle,
slouched on the curb,
     or strolling ribtight alleys
that ravel like twine;
    watching jewelers thrill metal
       to carve steel netsukes,
and handymen work miracles
     with stupefied wood;
   learning alien artforms and lingoes;
gaping at creatures
      gaping as spellbound at me,
   pirouette for pirouette,
our eyes fumbling one another
       like pubescent children;
   hearing traders gabble and sign
   an argot spiky as hieroglyphics
    moaned; talking shop
with gauchos from Aldebaran; clapping eyes
   on new and unimagined
     monotonies.

IV.   My heart's no émigré;
the glib traffickings of a squirrel
    can detain me for hours.
So, too, the mud runes left by a newt.
        I try my goodwill on resident aliens
            like the earthworm, or the apple.
    I know so little about an oyster's logic,
or why slugs mate acrobatically
            from slime gallows.
        Earth isn't small enough for me
to exhaust. Why covet mind-teasers
            lightyears away?

    A kennelled dog croons in my chest.
        I itch all over. I rage to know
    what beings like me, stymied by death
and leached by wonder, hug those campfires
            night allows,
        aching to know the fate of us all,
wallflowers in a waltz of stars.

V.

❧ *LANGUAGE LAB*

Doing Spanish, a young girl
resumes her lament, briskly,
in a blood-chilling monotone,
"My father is very sick,
he is growing thin and pale.
Yes, my mother is sick, too,
and we are terribly worried . . ."

For half an hour, a slim
marzipany voice renders color,
fruit and weather in French.
He orders lunch in a café,
then his mood sours. "I was hungry!"
he moans to his tape recorder
and, mispronouncing only one vowel,

says instead: "I had a woman!"
Sniggers from the Belgians
and Ghanaians. A black face
drifts round the booth wall
like a nimbus. "*Faim,* not *femme!*"
He wags a long finger.
"Bad trouble you mix them."

Hunched over a machine,
a Syrian mutters, "I am *not*
your sister. I am nobody's sister . . ."
A Bolivian boy waves
from a corner seat, his teeth
fiery in the bomb-bright neon.
"Hola, Diana!

How's your sick family today?"
His new English wobbles
like a first bicycle.
"Bout the same," I answer,
dragging off my headset,
"Mom's dying; dad's still
in that same auto wreck."

"I'm sorry, so terribly sorry,"
a Korean vows, as if telling
Hail Marys, "so sorry,
so terribly sorry, so sorry . . ."
while a spiky redhead repents
in Portuguese for all the heresy and lust
she looks forward to.

Only false gods rule
in this Babel of curt pleas
and one-syllable verbs,
where the heart's always blunt
enough to slap a noun on,
and, too willingly, the felt
dissolves in the sayable.

The room swells with an extra
Afghan, Thai or Swede.
And the occasional onlooker,
trying to make sense of it,
finds the world shrunk
to twenty-five bright islands,
an archipelago of madness and regret.

❧ CONCERT

Mildred, your light, steady hands
fill the house with music.
Ravishing, poignant piano sonatas
played to the basso whisper
of a cassette, one spring afternoon
in an English village, so many measures
across the deaf, ambiguous Atlantic.

At 85, your voice is tissue paper
as you announce the bill:
Handel, Beethoven, Haydn.
Then you stun us. Youth arcs through your fingers.
When you play, you are ageless.
Confident and lissome, when you play
you are 20 again, the butcher's daughter

and a concert pianist, on stage
when Victoria and Oscar Wilde reigned,
and before marriage sealed up
the short flue of your ambitions.
Fifty years more, you taught piano
for coin and barter, to every single child
in the cod and coal-dust town.

Grown up, how could they forget you?
All seasons, they still leave
cauliflowers and beetroots,
sacks of coal and kindling: anonymous tribute.

Perhaps even this tape, which you monogram
with Haydn's bouncing trills
and Beethoven's rigid lusheries,

mother's music for her son across the sea,
who visits all October, but always leaves you spooked.
Will this be the last time, but one?
You who feared the 20th Century, holding out
against fridge, phone, bank balance
and more, till you were a safe, cool 80,
send us the unlikeliest gift of a cassette.

Springtime. You are girlish.
Your hands spread wide as calipers
to capture the rugged angles of village life.
Mixed with the concert, your own complex notes.
We hear their sturdy counterpoint:
the ticker strong and guiltless,
the love without measure. Your touch is perfect.

❧ PATRICK EWING
TAKES A
FOUL SHOT

Ewing sweating,
molding the ball
with spidery hands,
packing it, packing it,
into a snowball's
chance of a goal,
rolling his shoulders
through a silent earthquake,
rocking from one foot
to the other, sweating,
bouncing it, oh, sweet
honey, molding it,
packing it tight,
he fires:

floats it up on one palm
as if surfacing
from the clear green Caribbean
with a shell
whose roar wraps around him,
whose surf breaks
deep into his arena
where light and time
and pupils jump
because he jumps

After months of pen-weary,
    gristle-pale verses, I bundled up
  against the onblast, drew a scarf
over the brain
      so blunted,
and, fearing my pigeon gift had flown,
    set out for the only work left me,

when I thought I saw Savonarola walking
    catty-corner across the quad,
      his hem a broom
  drafting the snow aside
as, pummelled by windfists, chin tucked,
    hands muffed in each sleeve,
      he strode toward the silent

chanting of two hawthorns, where high campus
    falls away,
  the winds curl, rip, bicker,
and on a near hill (eyeworthy even in fog)
    chinchilla-soft trees
    plush a hundred ways
under the air's turbulent palm.

    Savonarola trudged
along the maple row, where dry leaves chatter
    like a children's brigade. Behind him,
    the sun began setting in earnest,

grail-bright as it hugged the timberline.
A brown hood hid all
but his pulpit-large nose.

The belltower rang a dark note,
then moaned vespers.
Like a comet, a jet sighed white
across the sky.
Savonarola paused to fathom me.
And, as time became a fragrance,
I became a woman

caught up in the high, breaking fever
of an era, afraid
for my Rembrandts, not my soul.
Robe swishing,
he glided back into the quad,
his fury plain now
on the cave wall of his face,

and marched dead for me,
through hail
ranting down
like untold commandments,
toward me where I paled,
slab-cold on a step, already blinded
by the inquisition of winter light.

IN A PHILOSOPHER'S COTTAGE

FOR ALFONSO LINGIS

Below a quiver of Masai arrows
and a long, flexed bow whose resin
is drying out in central heat,
drying as the oiled limbs of its owner
never will in the sultry memories
a few photographs renew,

a lamp made only of an ostrich's left foot
and a single lightbulb
ghosts against an aquarium wall
where striped moray eels—bandannas with teeth—
and a lion-fish aflow with poison quills
swoop among blue coral mesas,
between shells brought from reefs
he's dived: the Great Barrier, Sri Lanka,
Yucatán, the Red Sea,
waiting for the live goldfish he feeds them
twice daily from a tank beside his bed,
or with chunks of frozen cod
his two, white, lavish cockatoos
fight over, perched on his shoulder,
while he guides us round the four corners
of his house, caressing neck feathers
and tufted yellow underwings,

taking care they catch no reflection
from the bathroom, mirrored like a discotheque,
with porcelain painted chrome,
a stuffed hammerhead shark twirling
at eye-level over the bathtub,
and two photos of Nehru drinking water by the door.

His collection of pinned Africans
under glass, butterfly and beetle,
he keeps in a room cool as a light thaw,
a tiny room where the deep-hued calligraphy
of antenna and wing incantates
among the plain, still angles.

There are lingam stones with fossil spirals
sealed within, a Zulu spear by the kitchen door,
where any Zulu would leave it,
mandalas in macabre detail and tints
only nature dyes so intensely
(and that only on frogs),
phallic carvings in ebony to resemble a pistol,
horned penis ornaments from Bali,
African batiks, a war mask from New Guinea
whose knee-length grey hair
charges the stairwell with static electricity,
knife-shaped books carved in Arabic
on palm leaves afray in the dry heat,
and given by young men from Kashmir or Calcutta,
a sacred jeweled Tibetan knife,
its blade forged from meteorite
(he winces when I touch it, sets it gently down),

fossilized rhinoceros teeth on rawhide,
a snakeskin vest from the ten snakes
whose livers he took with rice wine
in Tibet as a cure for impotence,
a typewriter beside a half-written essay
on causality, mother-of-pearl dinner plates,
anisette and cognac, a dozen photo albums he never
    shows.

Winter is a country he hasn't toured
for ten years. When he comes home, his life
is too eccentric to grasp: the months
spent picking vermin in a Thailand jail,
or deep in the exotic-erotica of Bali.
"How was your summer?" a colleague asks
who hasn't seen him for fifteen years.

Al has large, expensive picture books
of body ornament and regalia:
Leni Riefenstahl walking hand in hand
with a seven-foot Bantu, she in make-up,
bleached hair, and western clothes,
he in penis-thong and ochres;
they are strolling like any couple
on a hot Parisian evening, in paints and pomades.

Living among his artifacts,
he is living within his insides, turned inside out,
his house a form of body ornament
he applies inch by inch, its shaman rule
as unknown to bangled East as to suntanned West.

He pricks open his house,
fills a bole with ash, and then another,
until the raised marks connect into scars
dark as nightfall on the Kalahari,
scars winged, permanent and stiff, but chosen.

VI.

LINES WRITTEN IN A PITTSBURGH SKYSCRAPER

It has taken me three years
to come to this view.
I know now that the body
is a river, whose bones and muscles
and organs are flowing.
I have watched their shapes
in the molded Allegheny,
contained and onrushing, below bridge
after bridge vertebra to the Ohio,
a brown river that still
powers the mind, lying long
in the trestle arms of this city
whose sentence is hard labor.

Eye-level atop a church
across the street, St. Benedict the Moor
stands open armed and giant,
his back turned to the fuming
of a ghetto where some evenings
the brightest vision
is the flash of a streetlamp
on a jogger's white Nikes.

At night, the red sirens
spinning mute across the river
converge like pulsars
at some accident or crime.
An hour later, one pulls off,
hovers at a distance.
All is gesture and sign.

My students are the children
of coal miners, who watch the ground
swallow their fathers each day,
sometimes even digesting
the trapped men, turning their bones
back into lime, into coal.
It is the oldest fear:
that Earth may recall you.

Along the top of Mt. Washington
lies a stole of color
unnatural to sky. Twilight's blue collar.
But the mountains are a fishing
village: steep, hearty, and solid.
At night, the lights and stars

from my window make the cityscape
an Ethiopian bride. As cars bolt
around a curve of streetlamps,
their shadows flash from under them
like sprung souls. And the river
churning its wet whispery thighs,
the river pouring blood dark
under the bridges, in the river
I find my astonished limbs
and all the stateless gels within me,
carnal, mute, wholly flowing,
unburdened toward a distant shore.

❧ THE RUMORED CONVERSATION WITH ONESELF CONTINUES IN PITTSBURGH

and also a city with quiet pockets
stashed in the hubbub, like this one,

riverside at the base of the cablecars,
where we speak softly about time and space,

two rivers rushing from us as the Ohio does,
whose source is the Point we watch

from Frank's old Chevy, as warm Monongahela
and mountain-iced Allegheny merge blueblack

to vanish braided at the horizon.
What with ground glow, and flecks of city shimmer,

these water streets have more spangle
tonight than the sky. No meteors either,

though the Lyrids are past due.
The moon is nowhere; a hunch in the blackness.

Frank demonstrates its path on steeringwheel
and jutting stick-shift, telling the lunar opus

so deftly simple, I want to cry.
It's the way Pittsburghers play basketball,

or study Rilke: forging the rudest given
into calm, daily wages, mixing mill and bar

with the *Origin of Species*, discussing Proust
in the stands before a hockey match,

knowing the mind is a hard, slick muscle
toned by thought. And when I confess

that I've been thinking about cuffs all day,
how our joints are cuffs aswill with fluid,

and how the shape of cuff and bone-end
rule what sort, and how much, motion

will happen, and how the muscles
are bundles of string, across and through

and about the joints, at a twitch
hitching up the marionette of our bones,

for once I feel stark raving sane,
as we sit beneath the small lean-to of wonder,

letting our minds flicker quietly together.
We are talking about drift, our own,

and the continents' that clashed like stallions
to be Colorado or Tibet; how women

are marsupials; and early man thought fire
an animal he could only capture.

This is not an odd way to pass evening
in the largest inland riverport town,

but how strange to chat blithely about space
travel, in a Chevrolet whose back seat

sounds like a broken dinette set,
and mauled front seat looks driven to hysteria.

Across the river, a sandstorm of light:
buildings, arc lamps, staggering cars—

too dazzling for any one eyeful to snare.
Somewhere in the lit Oz of a city hospital,

a surgeon is breaking open the shrouded box
of a woman's chest, and reaching

a gloved hand into its snug, lonely muscle,
while she dreams of standing with Julius Caesar

across from the delta skyscrapers,
and barges, the train unzipping the night

at such speed, the tunnels and waterworks,
the time-and-motion boys, the computers,

and steam rising from the street vents,
rising from the single sweat gland

under the city, above which a million people
sleep through all the tiny lay-offs

in the cell, dream in the silent architecture
of nerve and bone, people who have not yet forgotten

how to wish, who are awed by the Space Shuttle,
but not by their own throbbing honeycomb of light

bridging three rivers and gyrating to eye's limit.
She would stand him, mouth agape,

under the moonless sky, across from night-burning mills
spewing raw fire back at the blackness,

across from a city whose incandescence
obscures even the most frantic stars.

❧ RIVER LIGHT

When boat lights flick on at dusk
the eye nimbly orders them
into constellations: a sky menagerie
as the fog roams in.
Arabs would have picked out
the ochre and the blue stars
naming them Fomalhaut, Rigel or Vega,
so nomads could spell their exile
with grains of light, and sense
even in the far-flung mazes of sand
other lids closing to the same lullaby.

Downstream, its steel paws
coated in river oil, a bridge arches
a sooty back against the night,
frozen in that delicate stretch forever.
Trinket small, a hefty machine
stands below, where it was left at 5 P.M.,
its limbs jutting out
like the crab of some metaphor
ready to pince life and drag it into view.

The men who work its arms
in the short hours after dawn
when blue does a veil dance
over the water, and sunlight throbs
each rivet into place,

in their private moments
away from the whistle-hoot and holler
do they love the architect of that bridge,
or what he loved?

*NIGHT ON
THE NILE*

Steep central among the bridges,
as if in the sternum
of a vast ribcage, the view
from my window is peril-less
and perfect: a stratagem
of lights that blacken the sky.

The city is lit, laid out, and still
like a jeweled Pharaoh
in the tomb of night.
There are neon talismans,
bandaged roads, and linen-wrapped girders
behind which small grimy beings
work at the testimonies of decay.

When a gold satellite
floats across the zenith at 10:00 P.M.,
it is the single thought
in the mind of a boy god,
a single mayfly of misgiving.

VII.

      GOLDEN SECTION,
      GIANTS STADIUM

I. The mind wakes to a whistle
     blown in the flesh, whose pea the mind is,
     wakes and flows down being's slipway,
     then *knows* the sheers of river light,
     bridge-rivets and factories,
     and raw, panting jungles so humid
     the snakes hang straight down, ghettos,
     and parkways where dogs salute trees
     and picnickers laze on gingham squares
     under the lightly buzzing stars.

     O the mind, the spidery mind
     on whose web the flies of meaning walk.
     Nature neither gives nor expects mercy,
     but the mind quests to be fit, to be seemly,

and fears second (dying is first)
to become just as plural as all it surveys.
So the autos of habit pull up
to each club at the prescribed hour.
So tidy moments of rapture unfold in the dark.
So the moon rises like a fat white god.

II. Who can know the dervish rhythms
of the mind that whirls for truth
in odd ports-of-call: a New Jersey stadium
whose dry surplus is autumn, late at night,
when the morse code of the galaxy
pales behind the fainter lights,
and, gifted with the breezy rhetoric
of his legs, a tall, willowy Beckenbauer
swivels, bluffs, and floats long passes,
running upfield among spoon-hipped Latins
playing soccer as if their sun could never cool.

Those tense men in mild weather
who hive and swarm, flying dense circles
around the ball's white flower
to ply the queen of wins with the honey
of their fatigue—for them, defeat lies
in the open scream of a goal-mouth,
and cheers rush like surf breaking
on the bony shoulders of their private sea.

Speak to me, Beckenbauer, about the rhythm
of the mind that searches for perfect order

in imperfect places: art galleries and polling booths,
books, sin-bins, and churches:
and can turn even ceremonial violence
to the mercy of a workable peace.

SOCCER AT
THE MEADOWLANDS

Near the goal, head sunk into his shoulders
    as he sprints, Chinaglia takes the ball
        spat at his feet,

dribbles it around a thatch of yellow shirts
    and, sliding between the legs
        of two defenders, belts it hard

into that caged, invisible *something*
    beyond the green reason of the field,
        in the netted calm no one enters.

The home crowd's ear-splitting rant
    grows seismic. Screams blur
        to wind howl and cymbals.

A jig-step. Chinaglia raises his fists
    as laurels. In a waking faint,
        he gallops round the pitch,

leaping, as if lovesick,
    into Marinho's arms, leaping
        to the hypnotic boom of the crowd.

❧ LOSING
THE GAME

On the face of this midfielder,
a saint's passion.

Sweat brilliantines his hair
flat as a seal pup's fur.

Thorns rake one knee, and fatigue
is a train whistle that never quits.

In his mind, the falcon of defeat
slips off its own hood

and sails into the vapory cold December,
hangs like a crucifixion over the field,

then slants down the wide thermal
of his shame. Today 2 + 2 is algebra,

and nothing will transmute
his base metal to gold leaf.

When crowd and players have gone,
he watches the sun set

under a tumultuous bruise of sky,
below the empty grin of the bleachers,

deep into the valley,
a ghastly, yellow bile draining out.

A VIEW
FROM THE
TERRACES

The American fans accepted me, but my
life was so quiet here that they never
really *knew* me.

> —Franz Beckenbauer,
> soccer player,
> at his farewell game

To know a dream, you must become the dream.
Your cloud-colored Mercedes.
The stadium lights glittering like Oz
in the distant smudge of a New Jersey evening.

The pain nimbus drifting from groin to thigh.
The handshake of a movie star
in a floodlit locker-room. The papal crowd roar.
The reporters trailing from each moment like vines.
The sobs and Lourdes-look of a fan.
The airport hours—tedium's long raga.
The freshet of victory. The $100 jeans.
The curfews. The endorsements for shoes
and shaving creams. The lifetime measured
in continental breakfasts. The tin promises.
The cool nights and hot women.

Sometimes, in a cricket-jazzed October,
we gather dark about us like an heirloom shawl,
content to have put up so many jars
of cactus-pear jelly, so many bottles of pickled beets,
and, in a mood clear as an oboe solo,
think how simply things can be known.
Porch slats. The tiptoe light of the stars.
Traces of oil shedding hallucination
in pond water by moonlight.
The remembered succulence of a broccoli stem.

But to know a deeper dream, the possibility
of dreaming, you must cease to dream,
and scrape culture off being's hot milk
(the one real dream we cannot know by dreaming).
Ingots straining on rubber: *Was that thunder?*
A willow-leaf's thin petiole: *Was that frailty?*
Purity's vengeance, a kernel scheming: *Was that mind?*
Like Salome, we dance with veils.

To 70,000 strangers in a packed arena
you whispered what lovers hurl
as the final reproach: *You never really knew me,*
and, for days, that blurted, tell-tale shot
burst from chamber to chamber inside me.
There are keener truths, I'm sure, leached
and drammed and ready for vials,
but no leaner hope, no older swansong.